Oz at Night

Other books by Amanda J. Bradley

Hints and Allegations, NYQ Books, 2009

Oz at Night

Amanda J. Bradley

N̲Q̲Y̲ Books™

The New York Quarterly Foundation, Inc.

New York, New York

NYQ Books™ is an imprint of The New York Quarterly Foundation, Inc.

The New York Quarterly Foundation, Inc.
P. O. Box 2015
Old Chelsea Station
New York, NY 10113

www.nyqbooks.org

First Edition

Set in New Baskerville

Layout and Design by Raymond P. Hammond
Cover Photo ©istockphoto.com/Yaroslav Osadchyy

Library of Congress Control Number: 2011937872

ISBN: 978-1-935520-45-0

Oz at Night

Acknowledgments

Grateful acknowledgment is made to the editors of the following journals in which these poems first appeared or in which they will soon appear: "The Nicene Creed Meets the Jabberwocky," *Gargoyle Magazine*; "Commodity Trading," "Stolen Identity," and "Oz at Night," *Paddlefish*; "To Thomas Pynchon Regarding *The Crying of Lot 49*," *Rattle*; "The Death of Stir Fry," *Lips*; "The Night Fred Lost It," *amphibi.us*; "A Description of Kant's Categorical Imperative in a Women's Clothing Catalogue" and "In the Days," *Playground Literary Journal*; "Upon Reading Berryman's Sonnets," *Best American Poetry Blog*; "Cups," *Pirene's Fountain*.

for my dear husband,
Ray

Contents

PART II: INVISIBLE THREAD

PART 1: RECKLESS STREAK

Blame it or praise it, there is no denying the wild horse in us.

~Virginia Woolf, from *Jacob's Room*

Let's Say...

Let's say the alligators one day crawled out
of the sewers of New York, blindly wreaking
havoc on the city, killing everyone in their
paths with chilling dexterity. Or let's say aliens
hovered over the city, menacing us for hours
and threatening in Morse code to exterminate.
Or let's say a psychic had informed you you'd be
hit by a bus the next day. Or let's say an asteroid
were hurling toward earth, predicted to strike
New York City and mottle our atmosphere,
killing the entire population. Or let's say Iran
got nuclear capability and fired at Israel,
so America fired back, starting World War III,
and we knew a warhead was hurling toward
NYC, with an hour's notice before the hit.
Or let's say one of us were incurably ill,
on our deathbed. What would our final
thought be? Would we say it?

Art Lessons

1.

My urge to slash and burn is back.
It's never out of style at large.
Too much maiming and not enough
forgiveness prove the constant plagues.
Who needs locusts? Today, my faith
in the importance of art is slipping.

2.

What is the overarching narrative?
What is the genre? What is my motivation?
Where should I stand when I say this?
There is nothing significant to say.
I could write words and words for another
ten years. Who would live differently?

3.

I ask repeatedly is your honesty so much
bullshit? You keep right on truth telling,
subtly, quietly. You might have something
in the action, the persistence. The most poignant
thing you have taught me today is the one
about trust—how it is slow, painful, worthwhile.

Upon Reading Berryman's Sonnets

What so sexy in a sonnet lurks?
Is it between the lines as legs or sheets
hide wonders lovers clamber to repeat,
or is it the tradition that it works?
Does language force the mental tongue embark
on crevices and larks that tempt to heat
the flush and pulse of skin that suffers sweet,
such lush and ample games of toward remark?

If you, my dear, would love me half as well,
your touch incline me to such ecstasies
as when I read the pain in what you write,
I would not rise from bed to answer hell,
nor salvage purity on bended knees,
and so, mindfuck me—please—through torrid night.

The Death of Stir Fry

I came back to our dorm room late, as usual,
to find my roommate waiting up for me,
not as usual. She asked me if I noticed
anything different. A quick, drunken scan
of the room revealed nothing: the usual
white Christmas lights around the ceiling,
the Pixies poster and Jack Nicholson's foot tall
evil grin in *The Shining*, the giant Jesus hand
sculpture we'd found at a yard sale, and the
retro-fifties clock on the wall. Everything seemed
in place. "It's Stir Fry," she said. "He died.
I came home, and he was floating on the surface."
I looked at the empty fishbowl on her desk.
Something about his absence and how solemn
she was, how sober and upset, the fact that she'd
waited up late to tell me the bad news made me
want to laugh. I struggled to stifle it. She told me
about the funeral and burial the next day,
what time it would be, as if I should send flowers
or wear black. She did wear black. I decided to
let it slip my mind. She didn't really want me there.

The Night Fred Lost It

The first hint was arriving home to find
all wall hangings removed and placed
under the bed face down. The second
was the call from a friend at Whole Foods
who said that he'd been fired. "Uh-oh,"
she worried. "Where is he?" Finally,
he arrived home, strange grimaces
and grunts menacing and emitting
from his face. "Are you okay?" she asked.
"Half my face is snoring because
I'm half asleep." "Oh," she replied.
"Where are your shoes?" she asked.
He shrugged. "What's in the bag?"
"Blue cheese," he said. "What for?"
she asked. "I collected all the blue
cheese in Evanston," he replied.
"Psychotropic," he said. "Maybe
we shouldn't have done so much
cocaine the last few days," she thought.
"Will you marry me?" he said.
She told him they could discuss it,
but shouldn't he get some sleep first?
He refused to go to bed or to listen
to anything but Jefferson Airplane
on vinyl. Eventually, he would take
a black marker and draw a large door
on the wall of the psych ward
in the state hospital with an EXIT
sign above it and try to walk through.

Suspicion

It scratches, erodes, abrades.
A faint tapping.
It falters and spies,
eats clues for lunch,
has properties of hope...
but is meaner.
A squinting of eyes.
A cold underbelly.
Dark gray and insidious,
it leaves one hanging
amidst traces and doubts.
One becomes skeptical,
cynical in its clutches,
a detective.
A little niggling thing,
it overshadows the obvious,
creates space, inspires.
It can be sexy and isolating.
It allows...

Sometimes at Night

Alone, I am
so in tune,
the universe
coursing
the circuitry
of my nerves,

I fear the proximity.

I cannot close
my eyes.
I brim with secret
knowledge.

It is unbearable,
the synchrony
too great
to sustain.

I feel schizophrenic,
torn between
two worlds,
visible and not.

The moment
must pass
from my simple
mind.

Please pass,
please pass,
I think,
my awe

enormous.

There's a planetary conspiracy...

What we once thought we had we didn't
and what we have now will never be that way again
so we call upon the author to explain.
~Nick Cave

Ask me who knows how this feels.
Gain my confidence. Scale that wall
Again. Be certain we are of the same
Ilk, glancing sideways, crabwise.
Nail that impression into us.
Snag hard-won trust. Laugh at the
Taint of irony, everywhere. Let
This hate whip frenzies and freeze
Hints in both of us. Look west and
East, but do not look up. You will
Lag behind. Open the gate this great
Instant of time sublime. Call us to
Kill in our sleep, in our waking, in
Elegies and odes and harangues that
Stain the ubiquity...of you and me.

Missing You

Spotted moon above
means nothing to me tonight
with you somewhere else.

Foghorns from New York
Harbor mimic my slow thoughts,
coming and going.

Light creeps through curtains,
covers me in my warm bed.
You are not here too.

I anticipate
what will never happen here,
and I have for years.

You continue to
punish me—perhaps you should.
I cannot let go.

A love that never
begins can never end, too.
Is that your reason?

Dropping You Off at the Train Station

As I left you there, I wanted to look back but knew you would not.

Your refusal would cause me more pain had I turned to see you
walking away. And knowing that, unlike Orpheus, and despite
our young love, you did not, was more than enough to bear.

It left me wondering how I could be so certain you did not turn and
whether it was a lack of desire to wave goodbye one last time
or a refusal to. And did a lack of desire indicate, I had to think,
that you didn't care enough or that I cared too much? And
did a refusal indicate, as I thought, a withholding on your part,
a habit of withholding that could not sustain my love? Yes,

it allowed fear to creep in so that I became like the dandelion
weeds lining the train track I observed once you'd left.
They were so close to being crushed by the train's weight,
and yet not quite close enough…

I wanted to not have to tremble every time the train left the station.
I wanted to be in the middle of a field, swaying free in the breeze.

Knowing my dandelion ways as I did, I knew I would be tempted
to grow tall enough and spindly enough to lay my delicate neck
on the metal beam.

I am sentimental. I spill over. I want to be allowed to push
and grow. Your withholding drives me crazy, ultimately
makes me sad and dangerous.
    It makes me want to die.

So I opted for the fields, where I can hear the distant train pass by.

22

Consent

I would have given you an arm's length permission and then

up close—if you'd wanted it, if you'd asked. You did not

have to move me. Back then and steadily moving forward,

I would have indicated, "You may do so in relation to me."

I would have granted you the right to step on my pedicured toes.

I would have accepted your intrusion into my days

and afternoons and evenings and nights. I would have

consented. But you did not ask. Rather, you took me

by surprise, and I have trouble forgiving that you did not

care if I wanted a pink rose for romance left on my door

or these messages carefully placed in my inbox, on my voicemail

like a puzzle: How could he know that? How could he?

It is not in my nature to hold grudges, but you give me

no choice. Your silence forces mine, and your imposing

will refuses my consent, no matter how I try to give it.

Grand Canyon

You say: "I want to jump in to feel myself falling,
one with the energy here." "That's creepy,"
I reply. "No it's not," you say, a smile slowly
forming beneath your distant eyes.
It disturbs me to hear your death drive at the surface.
Aren't I to be the one in tune with how to die,
ways to do it, little known methods like helium,
chances of coma versus death using this and that
medication for overdose? You are supposed to be
the one who finds my morbidity unsavory.
But I realize you have picked the one way
you would consider worthy. I am cheaper about it.

I am reminded of the movie *The Rapture,*
from the early nineties, starring Mimi Rogers.
Rogers plays a woman who eats a gun but is saved
by inspiration from God. Dedicating herself
to serving God's will, she does everything right
for years and years. She's a convert, a disciple.
She meets a cop who hasn't really thought much
about God at all. Eventually, God asks
her to kill her daughter, but unlike in Abraham's
case, He does not stay her hand. The rapture
comes, the cop smiles and disappears, but she is
angry. She can not forgive God for what He made
her do. She remains on earth, pissed and cast out.

Where is your struggle, I wonder. I admire
your peace, your acceptance that all will be
as it will be, your conviction if you leapt
here to your death, all would be well.
I lack that conviction. I suspect I always will.
I shake my fists, God forgive me. God forgive me.

Fluorescence

These caffeine-and-alcohol-animated,
ephedrine-fueled limbs make me feel
almost robotic as I aim to get more
coffee, more cream, more sugar
at the 7-Eleven at midnight or later.
If I were actually a robot, I would know
the precise time, aligned as I would be
with the atomic clock. Instead, the fluorescent
lights contribute to my impression that
I'm jerky, unsteady. Along the shelves
of the convenience store, I notice vitamin gumballs
then Doritos: Nacho Cheese, Nacho Cheesier,
Texas Paprika, Baja Picante, Zesty Taco Chipotle Ranch,
Blazin' Buffalo and Ranch, Guacamole!
The newness and variety of these products
make me think of bionic brain chips that will allow
paralyzed limbs to be moved by thought.
I am *deliberately* impaired. I could be
coming up with fabulous ideas: iPods,
digital cameras, in vitro fertilization,
screenplays, wireless, the slogan
"Secret: strong enough for a woman."
Instead, I throw back beverages, ingest pills,
smoke leaves, until my movements
are different and therefore interesting to me,
so that I feel alive and dead at once.

Come

I dress my lover's neck with a string of beads.
We drink gin martinis overlooking city streets,
creating something new from hidden needs,
saying things unexpected, indiscreet.

The morning sun reveals her face hid in her hair,
I know she wears my bra under her dress,
and I love moments when prudence is not called for
as giant, fleshy snowflakes press

us home, her one way and me another.
The end begins. I'll be her other lover.

My Red-Brown Hair

A wall of wind at my back,
I steer November streets,
cracked by Jack Daniels, no sleep.
Dive bar behind, I stride, fearless
as eighteen years ago, although
I know bad things come to those
who wait. I refuse to heed good
advice: my reckless streak—
an unfortunate trait. Raised in
eight cities, habitual moves
got in my blood. These circadian grooves
are flawed by the drive to go go go.
Don't test me. I'll just make you sad.
Home is not a word I know.

Gypsies are too tight-knit.
I feel kin with cowboys:
the open road, the grit
of no noise but coyote cries
and wind. In my element
anonymous or alone,
near imaginary tumbleweeds I sit
or rest my head on bone.
The country's wide and wild.
I don't buy the homestead bit.
I trust the moon's guise, its wily
gaze, its light, bent. I sin while
dust collects in my red-brown hair.
I've never been from anywhere.

INTERLUDE

Three be the things I shall have till I die:
Laughter and hope and a sock in the eye.

~Dorothy Parker, from "Inventory"

The Nicene Creed Meets the Jabberwocky

We believe in one Lord, Bandersnatch,
the only Son of Jabberwock,
eternally begotten of the Tumtum tree,
Jabberwock from Jabberwock, mimsy from mimsy,
true mome rath from true mome rath,
begotten, not uffish,
of one Being with the Bandersnatch.
Through him all things were frabjous.
For us and for our salvation
he came down from Callouh! Callay!
by the power of the vorpal blade
he became incarnate from the Jubjub bird,
and was made man.
For our sake he did gyre and gimble under manxome foe;
he suffered death and was snicker-snack.
On the third day he rose again
in accordance with the slithy toves;
he ascended into Callouh! Callay!
and is seated at the right hand of the Jabberwock.
He will come galumphing back to judge the living and the dead,
and his kingdom will burble as it comes.

We believe in the beamish boy, the giver of chortle,
who proceeds from the Jabberwock and the Bandersnatch.
With the Jabberwock and the Bandersnatch,
he is whiffled and frumious.
He has spoken through the outgrabe.
We believe in one holy gyre and gimble Church.
We acknowledge one burble for the forgiveness of brilligs.
We look for the galumphing back of the dead,
and the life of the tulgey wood to come. Amen.

Two Poets

for Ray

Two Poets Take Notes
Poet A: Where'd my pen go?
Poet B: I saw you put it down right there.
Poet A: Well, it's not there now, is it?
Poet B: Check your bag. Maybe you put it in your bag.
Poet A: I haven't touched my bag. It's not in my bag.
Poet B: You can borrow mine. It's around here somewhere.
Poet A: Oh, here's mine! It's at my feet.
Poet B: Where's our paper?

Two Poets Read an X-Ray for Kidney Stones
Poet A: I don't see anything.
Poet B: Maybe if we held it up to the light...
Poet A: Where's the kidney supposed to be?
Poet B: Somewhere in there, I think.
Poet A: I still don't see anything.

Two Poets Fold a Map
Poet A: Does it go this way first or this way?
Poet B: Just follow the creases.
Poet A: What do you think I'm trying to do?
Poet B: Give me that. I'll do it.
Poet A: Okay, Sherlock. You figure it out.
Poet B: This must go this way and then it folds here.
       Hm. Maybe not.

Two Poets Discuss Their Behavior
Poet A: I'm only being childish because my birthday is the
      last week in March, which is the first week
      of the Zodiac, the week of the child.
Poet B: I'm only telling you what to do because my birth
      date is the same date as Caligula's. I'm kingly.
Poet A: And a pervert.
Poet B: That too. What's my moon sign again?
Poet A: Cancer, which is a particularly strong placing because
      Cancer rules the moon.
Poet B: So I'm a nurturing pervert then.
Poet A: Exactly. And Cancer is *my* rising sign. I read once that
      Aries Sun Cancer Ascendant people should be lion tamers.
Poet B: I can actually see that.
Poet A: Yeah, me too.

Two Poets in a New York Apartment Decide What to Order for Dinner
Poet A: Thai?
Poet B: Mexican?
Poet A: Middle Eastern?
Poet B: Burgers?
Poet A: Sushi?
Poet B: Polish?
Poet A: Indian?
Poet B: Spanish?
Poet A: Chinese?
Poet B: Pizza!
Poet A: Pizza.

Cups

I. First Cup

I am half human.
Do not speak to me
until my nostrils
fill with bitter bliss,
stunning me to attention,
until my tongue,
furry with that
black intensity,
loosens from a land of
silence and vision—
a world I quickly
forget, sipping that
thin, watery nectar,
that elixir, that brew.

II. Second Cup

Jolted, I join
the land of the living.
The first intimations
that I might survive
this day after all
sink in, begin to
take hold. I am
mastered. I need
more of this joyous
juice. Sipping sends
me into great
awakenings, into
wild imaginings.
You may now speak to me.

III. Third Cup

Sneaking up on me,
caffeine crawls
through my veins,
its slender tentacles
reaching my outer
limits, hinting at
potential frenetic
energy, potential
loss of control,
driving semi-spastic
movements of my limbs.
An utter meltdown
or a bona fide eureka
is on the horizon.

IV. Fourth Cup

I reach a jittery crescendo.
Speech shoots forth
from my mouth
with freakish vehemence.
Words chase one another
like rollercoaster cars
racing downhill.
My forehead buzzes
as if my frontal lobe
were lit up, neurons
firing furiously.
Vociferous swilling
sweeps me into activity.
Oh glorious feeling!

To Thomas Pynchon Regarding *The Crying of Lot 49*

You wrote this slim volume and then I wrote one
hundred eleven pages about it in a dissertation
I abandoned. One hundred eleven seemed so
significant as I randomly landed there, those binary,
singular numbers lined up so neatly like three straws.
God damn you, Pynchon! You know, J. Kerry Grant's
companion to *Lot 49* notes you use the word
god thirty-three times in your novel. On purpose?
Was that on purpose?! I want to punch
your reclusive face. Where are you, Pynchon?
So, *I'll* use the word god here three times and then *you*
can decide to what extent or in what capacity
I may or may not believe in such notions as purpose
and entropy and preterite versus elect. By the time I was
done, I had underlined and starred in color-coded
markings nearly every sentence of both *Lot 49*
and its companion with comments in the margins
such as Irigaray? Lacan? Countercultural symptom?
Commodity fetish?—always ending with a question mark.
I told my advisor I'd write about all of your works,
but I got obsessed with underground postal systems
and Jacobean revenge tragedies, and Oedipa Maas and I?
We became one and the same! I was her in the flesh,
which does not refer to communion wafers metonymically,
unless it does so subconsciously, which it could,
I suppose. Anything's possible in your world, Pynchon.
You could mean so many things couldn't you?
You aren't just being cute, are you? You must mean
something. What do you want to point out here,
Pynchon? Why are you writing at all, Pynchon?

I read about the "massive axiological
catastrophe that provides the normative context
for this lived caricature of life" and wrote about the
"omni-contextual nature of reality and identity"
and said that some people accept a "consensual reality
over a solipsistic or a nihilistically paranoid one,"
but by page 111, I couldn't believe myself.

Running into Roy Batty and Pris at the Laundromat

Even tech noir stars have dirty laundry,
apparently, I think to myself as I try
not to stare at the lovely couple nearby.
"I want more life, fucker," Batty mutters
repeatedly as he loads the colors.
"That was a pretty good line, huh, Pris?"
"Yeah, whatever, Roy. Pass the detergent,
genius." Batty hands over the Tide,
tosses the last gray tee into the washer,
and slams the door. "Can you start this
thing, Pris? I can never remember how
to work them." Pris sighs, and I watch
as she glides her perfect pleasure model ass
over to him and sets the buttons and dials.
"It must be rough to be a pleasure model,"
I think. Batty glances in my direction,
as if he read my mind. I quickly look away,
afraid of his steel eyes. Outside, the cars
fly by overhead and reflections of neon
streak black, wet streets. I spot Deckard
peeking at them from behind a wonton stand.
Should I warn these two of the upcoming
chase scene and tell them how it all ends?
"If we wind up retired in a few days,
I think I have my last words worked out,"
I hear Batty say. "Nah, I'll let it play out
the way it should," I think. "Like tears in rain,"
Batty says, staring blankly at the trails
of water streaming down the windows.
Pris touches his shoulder lightly, cocks
her head at a strange angle and whispers,
"No one lives forever, Roy—no one."

A Description of Kant's Categorical Imperative in a Women's Clothing Catalogue

The colorful embroidery on this simple maxim reflects the sophisticated artistry of a man who spit out his meat after enjoying the taste of it. A magnificent, highly detailed enlightenment philosophy adorns the front, while epistemology tests the limits of the human ability to know, brightening the upper back. Exquisite sandwashed empiricism meets velvety soft rationalism with a flowing drape. A lightly crinkled version of the golden rule, the categorical imperative has a full-width zipper closure at the bottom back. Simply stated, if everyone wore a partial front placket with oversized shell buttons for a relaxed and polished look, would the world be better off or wanting an attractive, longer length?

Dear Journal,

I am leaving you. I used to write in you and then throw
you in the trash. Reading through my fourteen-year-old's
dedication to religion, I would throw you away.
Remembering, at your behest, my silly, bubbly scrawl
and the morons I had mooned over at sixteen,
I would deposit you squarely in the trash. I was wiser
in this respect when I was younger. I should listen to
my own counsel and toss the last eleven years of you
on a pyre. It is only because I don't reread you now
that you exist at all. All these years, I have confided
and confessed in you, and where has it gotten me?
Deep within, you always suggest. Well, yes, into
the depths of despair, I must respond. You drag me
to the heights of agony then make me wallow
in my own sniveling morass—the morass that you
created, journal—you, not me! You suggest I am
introspective and must work through my emotions
with you, alone, to prevent me from exploding
the scary stuff inside me to other, less tolerant friends,
but you, you should know...I am leaving you
for conversation. I am leaving you for interaction
and relation and healthy tête-à-têtes with real friends
who have my best interests at heart and don't require
full disclosure, who don't need to know my innermost
thoughts and feelings—the ones that you gnaw on
with your sharp, gnashing teeth. You're a bitch,
journal, and now I can finally see it. Good riddance.

Sincerely,
Amanda

Mind of Night

Whose thoughts colonize my dreams?
Beings I fear I'll witness somersaulting the sky
above, their inner lights bright like café windows
signaling my unconscious to act I know not how.
I do not understand this deep desire for
connection though I sense their sentience,
their wisdom of fools, threading language
through thought and dream images nightly
of lands unseen and slaughtered animals,
tapping my already fragile mind of night.
What sage creatures make these simple demands—
the center of my question for them, knowing,
though, I can barely withstand this sad intrusion.
Through complex neuron firings, they show realization
that poetry shimmers in people like me
who grew up taking stock of the world around them.
Reading imaginative stories all my life, I am
defenseless against such mental inhabitations
as they sit on their stars and look down.

Tell me something.

Jesus Was a Leo

They set Christmas over the Jewish holiday
to eradicate the old as the Jews set Hanukkah
over Winter Solstice celebrations
and for the same reason. Yet Jesus is still
a Capricorn to many. Wandering the stacks
at the library in college, a book title caught
my eye: *Jesus Was a Leo*. I presume it was
about how unlikely it is that Jesus was born
on December 25 from an historical perspective,
but perhaps it suggests that Jesus was a natural
leader and a generous, loyal person like Leos are.
Makes sense to me. Why not a Leo?

George W. Bush claimed Jesus Christ is his
favorite philosopher, although he flagrantly
ignored his teachings on poverty and his
"Blessed are the peacemakers." Google Jesus
and poverty and your first hit is "Was Jesus a Marxist?"
A more easily answered question than
"How can people actually believe that Bush
has the teachings of Jesus in his heart?"
I used to accept Jesus as my personal savior.
I was baptized—twice—once as an infant
Lutheran and again as an adolescent Baptist.
I was officially confirmed, and my godparents
gave me a white Bible with my name engraved
on it and a cross bookmark. I taught
Vacation Bible School in Texas.

But Jesus is not *my* favorite philosopher.
He had a lot of important stuff to say,
at least according to the people
who wrote it down 70 to 100 years after
he supposedly said it. At least in the translations
to English that are available. It's a powerful
story, granted. What's more amazing than water
to wine and all that, though, is that people
have killed in the name of this peaceful man
for centuries and centuries, that today
people insist we should elect Republicans
as good Christians. But Republicans benefit
the rich. Do those kind-hearted Christians
not care about the poor more than another
tax break? Isn't it just that simple?

PART II: INVISIBLE THREAD

I am no lover of disorder and doubt as such. Rather do I fear to lose truth by this pretension to possess it already wholly.

~William James, from *The Varieties of Religious Experience*

Courage

I thoroughly believe in explanations.
I do believe it's this way or that way.
But this way could be all of the above,
and that way could be infinitely so.
It seems to me it has to be the way it is.

It's rare we can access the truths
we wonder most about. Like a leaf
dangling from an invisible thread,
truth taunts us in its dance.

At least we know that time relents
with its additions and subtractions,
sleep and death. There is wisdom
in knowing a fearless courage
will allow you to blow down a door
and through the house and out
a crack in the window.

Aftermath

It was good to live in Chicago again,
down the street from my pal.
We dawdled on the patio
at the Happy Village Bar
drinking gin and tonics with lime
and hoped her current boyfriend
might really build a house
on a plot of land he owned
in Mexico. There, we could
live in retirement, baking
in the trenchant sun.
She capriciously suggested
we would listen to an audio copy
of *Finnegan's Wake.* I would
order cases of tequila
to be brought to the house.
We'd smoke cigarillos on Saturdays,
memorize episodes of *Twin Peaks,*
and fill the house with birds.
Our friends would come to visit
and never leave, and musky perfumes
from musty bodies would rise
through the house to permeate
the top floors. In Chicago,
I knew the neighborhoods
and streets as in no other city.
I regularly walked to the Art Institute
to see Picasso's *The Old Guitarist.*
I hoped to be that old, to make it that far,
to be writing still, with white hair
and twisted limbs, sunken cheeks
and wrinkled face. I wanted to remain
aware of the blueness of life.
Chicago was all about the blues.

Only Imagined

Why can I feel this person's fingers
strike this keyboard? Who is she sitting
where I sit, thinking what I think?
How can she claim to be me? I am
foreign, I am alien, I am not me.
She took a walk before she sat down.
I was there, too. Abstractions filled
our mind, fleeting and fantastic—
awe at life, the fact of it, confusion.
Concrete things, too: "Look at that puffy
bird perched on the bench back."
"I am thirsty." Yet we're not grounded.
We are not together. She has lived a life
I have only witnessed. I have felt emotions
she has only imagined. One of us dreams
while the other sleeps, and every once
in a while, like now, we realize our separation.

Philosophy

Life is full of whimsy,
all things contingent
on caprice, malice.
Our fortunes unpredictable,
we bandy about,
not knowing from where
we came nor to where we go.
Philosophy is a choice
we make, a master.
It tells us change
is natural and more.
It whispers calm good
nights in our ears
when rain falls.
It speaks no evil
because evil is unreal,
a contrast, a mere idea.

The Source

"Make it new," said Pound.
He had a fascist sensibility.
And then so did much
of Europe. Some things
can be taken too far,
as the spirit of innovation.
Progress by any other name
would smell as sweet.
But then, is it even
expedient to conserve
the species? Death drives
us like Eros. With patricide
and infanticide, genocide
and suicide, with murderous
impulses, we rule this world.
Our strongest spirits
are also our most evil,
so why do we turn
to them for answers?

Stolen Identity

Do you ever get the sense
you don't know
what's going on?

Some streets I walk
in fear, aware
that satellite imaging
details my path and
security cameras
on poles holding
traffic signals record
where I wander,
all around the city.

I walk past a movie crew
setting up for shots,
past bodegas with
newspapers in seven languages
detailing military operations
in places I've never been and
medical miracles I can barely
conceive—face transplants,
cloning. I'm gripped by a sudden
compulsion to know more,
to talk to someone
on my cell phone.

I am hidden, anonymous,
disconnected as night settles
and the moon glints
like a giant white dot
on a screen in a shop window.

In the Days

Before city lights sprawled the spans of lands,
before red hues covered our landscapes, cloud-like,
when smog only smothered the City of Angels
and landfills only littered some outskirts,
when we trod barefoot over sand dunes and
backpacked trails through mountains,
before we'd lost accidents and happenstance
to structure, plans, rules, designed
to control ever more unruly elements,
when we were imperfect in each other's eyes
and love sprang up in spite of those
imperfections, because we could tear
at each other's differences, because we
could ruin one another in words, but chose
not to—from love, not from loathing—
those were the days we would fear nothing.

I am not what I would like to be nor what I will become

I am not an Olympic swimmer. I hold no unbending principles.
I am not Matt Damon, nor someone who carries an alligator purse.
I do not make up my mind easily. I do not like the limelight.
I do not care enough about the right things. I am not a monk.

I would like to be Beatrice in *Much Ado about Nothing* or an owl.
I would like to be present at events of interest that have already happened.
I would like to be someone who refuses to regret—successfully.
I would like to never dream about jewelry again or religious imagery.

I will become an old woman with osteoporosis and arthritis, God willing.
I will have bad knees. I will still have my scars. As every year already,
I will be less certain. If I am not too happy, I will write poems.
I will become someone I am not now, which I would like.

Home

I arrive in Indianapolis from New York City.
Almost immediately, I am ushered to my niece's
graduation from preschool. There are many
small people and babies. There are silly songs
and teachers shedding tears as they lead prayers
and tell the small people goodbye. I find myself
singing along: "Father Abraham had many sons,
and many sons had Father Abraham."
What about daughters, I think, as I sing this song
I know from my own childhood. I am turning
in circles, waving my arms, and kicking my legs
when they ask the audience to participate.
There is a large picture of dear Sarah on a wall
in a slideshow with a sign around her neck
saying, "When I grow up, I want to be a mommy."

At home, my apartment has walls lined with books.
A few plants are the only things I must keep alive.
It is quiet. I do not perform for anyone there.
Sometimes there is jazz. Sometimes my husband
and I play Scrabble or watch a movie. When I
go out, it is to a poetry reading, a museum,
to take a walk to the park by the ocean.

Raccoon

In college, reading *Crime and Punishment,*
I asked my friends what they would do
if I confessed to them alone that I had murdered
someone. Some: "It would be our secret."
Others: "I would turn you in." Some proved
philosophical: "It would depend on whom
you had killed in what situation, on why."

You fell in the philosophical camp,
genuinely torn between loyalty
and conscience, contemplative
about what situations warranted loyalty.

Remember when we saw a badly injured
raccoon near the road? In the moment,
I recalled my brother and his story
of breaking the neck of the deer he'd hit
to put it out of misery. Remember I told
you that you should kill the raccoon,
that it was the compassionate thing to do,
as if I knew what I was talking about?

You got out of the car that I pulled
to the side of the road, and you chased
it down, beat it over and over again
with a rock until you were certain.

What I didn't think was that my brother
is a hunter and carries a baseball bat
in his SUV just in case, whereas you
proudly tell the story of turning the other
cheek when a bully attacked you,
asking him if he felt better now.

Figuring out the right thing to do
proves impossible most of the time,
and trying too hard gets in the way.
The memory of the deer probably
makes my brother proud now,
and the memory of the raccoon
makes you shudder, I would imagine.
And the memory of who would have
had my back no matter what makes
me proud and makes me shudder too.

This Condition

there's little we know
alone in our minds' traps
fleeting and doomed
a single firefly glow
afraid of evil and accidents
longing for the inaccessible
the forgotten
inscrutable

and yet...
something guides us
if only our imaginations
our inability to stop
the sun from rising

Context

This morning I woke
to the sound of laughter.
Was that me or my lover,
I wondered as I reached
the surface. Laughter
without context unnerves.

Grace Poole rushed to mind,
how she was blamed for
Bertha's laugh in *Jane Eyre*
and how creepy I'd found that
when I was young—
her laugh, her prowling about
at night with a candle,
starting fires.

Drinking Water

We vanish behind computers
and apartment windows
with sheer curtains, noticing
how indiscriminate nature is,
how rabid and how delicate.
More hermits every year,
we put on a good show
watching leaves change and fall
and sprout and dry and change.
We are everywhere now
like ants with our elaborate cities.
We are everywhere now,
and nature is indiscriminate,
taking us out by the thousands
with one rumble of ground,
rush of water, roar of wind.
We watch how fragile we are,
and we feel ourselves signifying
nothing behind our screens
and our curtains wondering
who to trust with our money
to get those people, those
who survive, drinking water
because they are everywhere
and we are everywhere too.

Southern Nightfall

A skinny dog scrounges for scraps by the old RC Cola Warehouse. An ancient magnolia tree shades the street littered with tiny rocks, waving carelessly above cars that poke by. Blues croons light lazily out windows through the thick summer air, still warm as evening encroaches. A neon light flickers on, the switch flipped inside the corner store. Popsicle juice slides down a young boy's brown hand as he kicks a rubber ball to his brother. Grandmothers and mothers take their seats on porch chairs now that dinner dishes are done. They light cigarettes and slowly inhale. The waning crescent moon slides behind clouds that promise rain. An owl hoots, and a pigeon darts for cover.

Catharsis

I understand how solving riddles
whets your drive to know.
I understand your blustering
ways, your billowing anger
the closer you grow to reaching
truth about the lot you've drawn
in life. You learn that bad shadows
good and ignorance knowledge,
that actions bring consequences,
often unjust. You learn that life
does not give us reason or rhyme.
It does not give us the wisdom
of gods, so we assume we only
know part of the scheme. Our drive
to make patterns is vast as we try
to make sense of life's crass ways.

But we, brave Oedipus, will not
wander plains in exile. The answers
we seek elude us. There is no moral
to this farce, our lives. And we
know it in our bones.

Carl Andre's *Equivalent V*

no mortar binds
these fire bricks,
meant to hold flame,
an American building block
for kilns and furnaces
brought to meaning
by breaking
sculpture's plane—
horizontal, horizontal, horizontal
the artist is not apparent
in abstraction of blue collar
work and math
one onlooker's
"pile of bricks"

Hunter Mountain

Glancing up the mountain, I see wide stripes of green
in a subtle, seemingly aimless zigzag down the sides
of Hunter Mountain between the bright and burnt
orange of leaves still on the trees. A ski slope makes
a strange sight this time of year. If you didn't know
what caused it, from a distance, a meticulous fire might
come to mind or another freak accident of nature, knowing
as we do the tricks she'll pull in the name of magnificence.

Six Days

I had six days with no news:
no watching, no listening to, no reading
accounts of catastrophes
and scandals and natural disasters.

Rather, I wandered about
my apartment, my neighborhood,
reading fiction, poetry, and emails
about personal lives, concentrating more
on depth than breadth.

I felt the weight of being here
at all, noticed the leaves on my house plants
browning at the edges, heard pigeons
cooing on the sidewalk below, appreciated
Dickinson's wicked sense of humor,
contemplated heaviness, felt silence.

More or less aware of my mortality,
unrushed by a sense of obligation,
I began to feel like someone
better: less forgetful, frenetic, pushed.
People say the human spirit
of innovation keeps us moving forward,
progressing, but I wonder
how a simpler world would feel
where we ran dirt through our fingers
and drank water more than wine,
watched as trees developed rings
and roots over years and years and years.

What We Know

The present blows us quickly by.
It's passing as you read.
It doesn't heed your wish to pause.
It doesn't feel your need.

To it, the longest lives are short,
the shortest lives the same.
It doesn't really matter much
what happens in between.

The only little thing we have
in any very minute
is our memory of the past
and what is passing to it.

And yet we sense that something matters
in the quickening of our lives,
so we don't just flick about
or toss the carving knives.

In much we strive for dignity,
caring as we go,
but we fail at it miserably
because of what we know.

Recollections

I have one memory as a toddler—
busting my lip on the pavement
on wobbly, unsure legs.
That was so long before I knew
what my problems would be.
How can I have been alive
so long and recall so little?

What I tend to remember most
are the character builders,
not the conversations with pals
outside on dry summer days,
not spontaneous laughter
with someone I love. Rewind.
Show me why we matter.

Growing Up with *Star Wars*

A child of the 70s, I found Luke more compelling
than Han Solo. Earnest attempts to learn the ways

of the force from Yoda reminded me of my own
attempts not to feel insignificant holding my mother's

hand at the supermarket. I did not collect the action
figures, but I had an R2-D2. His blips and beeps amused

me as a child, and C-3PO was a loquacious dork. I liked
that Luke slowly became more capable and sure of himself.

I hoped that Luke and Leia would hook up, was shocked
to discover they were brother and sister. Darth's deep

voice between mechanized breaths: "I am your father."
What a dynasty! Being selected from obscurity

into a meaningful destiny rules many lives, no matter
what story is at its root. But I'd always preferred to be

a jedi to a princess. When I learned I could get pregnant,
I was furious for ten years. All my warrior instincts

wasted in this pregnable body. Today, Han is much sexier
with his slapdash ways. Luke whines too much, as I suspect

I did too, back in the day. I'll never tire of watching
the original three movies. I still want to believe good will

beat out evil. That the battle rages grows more apparent
as I age. And for good to win becomes more important.

Oz at Night

A tornado rips fields into clots of blood.
The yellow brick road is beneath my feet.
Evaporating chills of winter whip
past and through me as one last declaration.
Night feels like a blue touch in my long hair.
Would Kandinsky love the colors of Oz
or would he find them banal, scattered, suffused?
I can't find her ruby slippers, though I know
they should be here somewhere, sparkling.
They must be long gone, lost in the prop
room or dusted in a Hollywood museum.
"We're not in Kansas anymore, Toto."
Everyone talks to their dogs. It's alright.
The primary colors of Dorothy's story
written on our collective unconscious make
us substantial as newspaper clippings and as thick.
I clicked my black sneakers and disappeared.
Amanda was gone, Oz lost in a moment of joking.
Play will destroy by accident.
Back to the sugary moon, back to the dirt.
I'll never get back to where I am going.
Il y a une horloge qui ne sonne pas:
even as you grow old and the world speaks
more openly and frequently and clearly to you.
You lie down on the bloody land, and it closes
over your face and limbs to say goodnight.

To Myself at Eighty

Are you still here?

You have better
habits than I.
But do you still like
rye bread and gouda
cheese and dark chocolate
like your grandmother?

Your elders must be dear
memories to you now—
and distant. Do you
hope to see them soon?

I wonder how your doubt
feels. Do you prefer long
walks and seclusion?

Do you regret
the things I suppose?
Remember how people
told you how courageous
you were when you
only felt a coward?

Does your life still
seem to you like
layers of irony piled
up like years?

You still, despite that,
strive to cull sincerity,
genuineness from each day.

You still surround
yourself with red pillows,
good friends, more books
than your space should hold.

You like pictures
of people you care for.
You wish you could recall
more specifics of the years.

You know how Ray
tells poets not to ask
too many questions
in their poems.
Do you heed his advice?

Do you still laugh?

Commodity Trading

I drag moments, days, months, years, like a collection
of short stories, behind me. But they don't slow me
down. Their residue has more weight, tugs at my coattails
like a nineteenth-century beggar. We don't touch
as much as we used to and yet we touch more.
Less is in the closet. Or are new things there?
More stuff, certainly: clothes, gadgets, food in the pantry,
books on the shelves, but that, too, is fading. Die,
capitalism, and quickly. You erode us, make us more and more
ironic, our stories less palpable, less sincere.
What purchase do we have in love, in friendships
with you always selling the farm, always turning moments
into collections of short stories, books of poems, careers?

Will

I'll just put a period on this sentence,
and it will end.

The struggle will prove less Herculean
than for some.

The fight will be a myth, as a lifetime
feels anyway.

I'll put this raggedy life to death,
smooth jagged edges.

The addling will be gone, scrambled eggs
in the trash.

I will shed no tears. I will break no backs.
Simple. I will.

photo by Brian Adams

Amanda J. Bradley's first book of poems, *Hints and Allegations,* was released in 2009 from NYQ Books. *Oz at Night* is her second book of poems. She has published poetry in many journals including *The Best American Poetry Blog, Paddlefish, Lips, Rattle, The New York Quarterly, Poetry Bay,* and *Barefoot Muse.* Amanda is a recent graduate of the MFA program at The New School, and she holds a PhD in English and American Literature from Washington University in St. Louis. She lives in Brooklyn.

About NYQ Books™

NYQ Books™ was established in 2009 as an imprint of The New York Quarterly Foundation, Inc. Its mission is to augment the *New York Quarterly* poetry magazine by providing an additional venue for poets already published in the magazine. A lifelong dream of NYQ's founding editor, William Packard, NYQ Books™ has been made possible by both growing foundation support and new technology that was not available during William Packard's lifetime. We are proud to present these books to you and hope that you will continue to support The New York Quarterly Foundation, Inc. and our poets and that you will enjoy these other titles from NYQ Books™:

Barbara Blatner	*The Still Position*
Amanda J. Bradley	*Hints and Allegations*
rd coleman	*beach tracks*
Joanna Crispi	*Soldier in the Grass*
Ira Joe Fisher	*Songs from an Earlier Century*
Sanford Fraser	*Tourist*
Tony Gloeggler	*The Last Lie*
Ted Jonathan	*Bones & Jokes*
Richard Kostelanetz	*Recircuits*
Iris Lee	*Urban Bird Life*
Linda Lerner	*Takes Guts and Years Sometimes*
Gordon Massman	*0.174*
Michael Montlack	*Cool Limbo*
Kevin Pilkington	*In the Eyes of a Dog*
Jim Reese	*ghost on 3rd*
F. D. Reeve	*The Puzzle Master and Other Poems*
Jackie Sheeler	*Earthquake Came to Harlem*
Jayne Lyn Stahl	*Riding with Destiny*
Shelley Stenhouse	*Impunity*
Tim Suermondt	*Just Beautiful*
Douglas Treem	*Everything so Seriously*
Oren Wagner	*Voluptuous Gloom*
Joe Weil	*The Plumber's Apprentice*
Pui Ying Wong	*Yellow Plum Season*
Fred Yannantuono	*A Boilermaker for the Lady*
Grace Zabriskie	*Poems*

Please visit our website for these and other titles:

www.nyqbooks.org

www.ingramcontent.com/pod-product-compliance
Lightning Source LLC
LaVergne TN
LVHW011429080426
835512LV00005B/350